HOW TO BE FILLED
WITH THE HOLY SPIRIT

including ·

FILLED WITH THE
SPIRIT . . . THEN WHAT?

HOW TO BE FILLED WITH THE HOLY SPIRIT

A.W. Tozer

Including

FILLED WITH THE SPIRIT . . . THEN WHAT?

R. Mabel Francis

CHRISTIAN PUBLICATIONS, INC.
CAMP HILL, PENNSYLVANIA

Christian Publications, Inc.
3825 Hartzdale Drive, Camp Hill, PA 17011-8870
www.cpi-horizon.com
www.christianpublications.com

Faithful, biblical publishing since 1883

How to Be Filled with the Holy Spirit including
Filled with the Spirit . . . Then What?
ISBN: 0-87509-924-6
LOC Control Number: 2001-131293

CONTENTS

Introduction vii

How to Be Filled with the Holy Spirit

A.W. Tozer

Preface xi

1 Who Is the Holy Spirit? 1

2 The Promise of the Father 15

3 How to Be Filled
  with the Holy Spirit 31

4 How to Cultivate the Spirit's
  Companionship 45

Filled with the Spirit . . . Then What?

R. Mabel Francis

Foreword 59

1 Am I Really Anxious for
   a Life of Victory? 61

2 Do I Hold the Idea That
   I Am Complete in Myself? 67

3 Is It Good Advice That
   I Should "Crucify" Myself? 73

4 Does God Deal with Aspects
   of the Self-Life in Children? 79

5 How Can I Show God That
   I Really Want to Please Him? 85

6 What Can I Do about a
   Chronic Lack of Patience? 89

7 What Makes Me Nasty and
   Unpleasant to Others? 95

8 What If I Have a Hypersensitive,
   Suspicious Nature?. 101

9 What about False Rumors
   Affecting My Reputation?. 105

10 How Can I Know That Self
    Has Gone to the Cross? 111

11 What May Be the Most Difficult
    Lesson en Route to Victory? 117

12 When Can I Expect Full Victory
    over Self? 121

INTRODUCTION

How to Be Filled with the Spirit and Filled with the Spirit . . . Then What? are two classic works that have deserved to be together for a long time. A.W. Tozer and Mabel Francis were contemporaries who at times undoubtedly ministered on the same platform. They have now gone on to their rewards.

I heard them both and was blessed by them both. They were godly people. They exalted Jesus Christ and walked in the power of His Spirit. Now, in this volume, they minister once again to the same audience at the same time.

In both cases, their legacy was a life well-lived in kingdom endeavor. These works merit your reading.

K. Neill Foster
December 2000

How to Be Filled with the Holy Spirit

A.W. Tozer

PREFACE

The following pages represent the gist of a series of sermons given on successive Sunday evenings to the congregation of the church of which I am pastor. The talks were taken down stenographically and later reduced to their present length. A fifth message which was a part of the series has been omitted here.

The fact that these were originally spoken messages accounts for their racy style and for the personal references which occur in them occasionally. Had I been writing the messages I should have exercised greater care in the composition. The subject is, however, so vitally important that I feel sure the reader will pardon the offhand style of the language. The truth is always good even when the vehicle in which it rides is homely and plain.

This book is made available to the Christian public with the prayer that it may help to lead many thirsty believers to the fountain of living waters.

— A.W.T.

CHAPTER ONE

WHO IS THE HOLY SPIRIT?

We all use the word "spirit" a great deal. Now I want to tell you what I do and do not mean by it. In the first place, we rule out all of the secondary uses of the word "spirit." I do not mean courage, as when we say, "That's the spirit!" I don't mean temper or temperament or pluck. I mean nothing so nebulous as that. Spirit is a specific and identifiable substance. If not definable, it can at least be described. Spirit is as real as matter, but it is another mode of being than matter.

We are all materialists to some extent. We are born of material parents into a material world; we are wrapped in material clothes and fed on material milk and lie in a material bed, and sleep and walk and live and talk and grow up in a world of matter. Matter presses upon us obtrusively and takes over our thinking so completely that we cannot speak of spirit without using materialistic terms. God made man out of the dust of the ground, and man has been dust ever since, and we can't quite shake it off.

Matter is one mode of being; spirit is another mode of being as authentic as matter.

Material things have certain characteristics. For instance, they have weight. Everything that is material weighs something; it yields to gravitational pull. Then, matter has dimensions; you can measure the thing if it is made of matter. It has shape. It has an outline of some sort, no matter whether it is a molecule or an atom or whatever it may be, on up to the stars that shine. Then, it is extended in space. So I say that weight, dimension, shape and extension are the things that belong to matter. That is one mode of being; that is one way of existing.

One power of spirit, of any spirit (for I am talking about *spirit* now, not about the Holy Spirit), is its ability to penetrate. Matter bumps against other matter and stops; it cannot penetrate. Spirit can penetrate everything. For instance, your body is made of matter, and yet your spirit has penetrated your body completely. Spirit can penetrate spirit. It can penetrate personality—oh, if God's people could only learn that spirit can penetrate personality, that your personality is not an impenetrable substance, but can be penetrated. A mind can be penetrated by thought, and the air can be penetrated by light, and material things and mental things, and even spiritual things, can be penetrated by spirit.

What Is the Holy Spirit?

Now, what is the Holy Spirit? Not *who*, but *what*? The answer is that the Holy Spirit is a Being dwelling in another mode of existence. He has not weight, nor measure, nor size, nor any color, no extension in space, but He nevertheless exists as surely as you exist.

The Holy Spirit is not enthusiasm. I have found enthusiasm that hummed with excitement, and the Holy Spirit was nowhere to be found there at all; and I have found the Holy Ghost when there has not been much of what we call enthusiasm present. Neither is the Holy Spirit another name for genius. We talk about the spirit of Beethoven and say, "This or that artist played with great spirit." The Holy Spirit is none of these things. Now what is He?

He is a Person. Put that down in capital letters—that the Holy Spirit is not only a Being having another mode of existence, but He is Himself a Person, with all the qualities and powers of personality. He is not matter, but He *is* substance. The Holy Spirit is often thought of as a beneficent wind that blows across the Church.

If you think of the Holy Spirit as being literally a wind, a breath, then you think of Him as nonpersonal and nonindividual. But the Holy Spirit has will and intelligence and feeling and knowledge and sympathy and ability to love and see and think and hear and speak and desire the same as any person has.

You may say, "I believe all that. You surely don't think you are telling us anything new!" I don't hope to tell you very much that is new; I only hope to set the table for you, arranging the dishes a little better and a little more attractively so that you will be tempted to partake. Many of us have grown up on the theology that accepts the Holy Spirit as a Person, and even as a divine Person, but for some reason it never did us any good. We are as empty as ever, we are as joyless as ever, we are as far

4

from peace as ever, we are as weak as ever. What I want to do is to tell you the old things, but while I am doing it, to encourage your heart to make them yours now, and to walk into the living, throbbing, vibrating heart of them, so that from here on your life will be altogether different.

Who Is the Holy Spirit?

So the Spirit is a Person. That's *what* He is. Now *who* is He?

What the creeds say

The historic church has said that He is God. Let me quote from the Nicene Creed: "I believe in the Holy Ghost, the Lord and Giver of life, Which proceedeth from the Father and the Son, and with the Father and the Son together is worshiped and glorified."

That is what the Church believed about the Holy Ghost 1,600 years ago. Let's be daring for a moment. Let's try to think away this idea that the Holy Spirit is truly God. All right. Let's admit something else into the picture. Let's say, "I believe in one Holy Ghost, the Lord and Giver of life, who with the Father and the Son is to be worshiped and glorified." For the "Holy Ghost," let's put in "Abraham, the father of the faithful, who with the Father and the Son together is worshiped and glorified." That is a monstrous thing, and in your heart already there is a shocked feeling. You couldn't do it. You couldn't admit a mere man into the holy circle of the Trinity! The Father and Son are to be worshiped and glorified, and if the Holy Spirit is to be included here He has to be equal to the Father and the Son.

Now let's look at the Athanasian Creed. Thirteen hundred years old it is. Notice what it says about the Holy Spirit: "Such as the Father is, such is the Son, and such is the Holy Ghost." Once more let's do that terrible thing. Let's introduce into this concept the name of a man. Let's put David in there. Let's say, "Such as the Father is, so also is the Son, and such is the hymnist David." That would be a shock like cold water in the face! You can't do that. And you can't put the archangel Michael in there. You can't say, "Such as the Father is, such also is the Son, and such is the archangel Michael." That would be monstrous inconsistency, and you know it!

I have told you what the creeds of the church say. If the Bible is taught otherwise, I would throw the creeds away. Nobody can come down the years with flowing beard, and with the dust of centuries upon him, and get me to believe a doctrine unless he can give me chapter and verse. I quote the creeds, but I preach them only so far as they summarize the teachings of the Bible on a given subject. If there were any divergency from the teachings of the Word of God I would not teach the creed; I would teach the Book, for the Book is the source of all authentic information. However, our fathers did a mighty good job of going into the Bible, finding out what it taught, and then formulating the creeds for us.

What the hymnists say

Now let's look at what our songwriters and our hymnists believed. Recall the words the quartet sang this evening:

Holy Ghost, with light divine,
Shine upon this heart of mine.

Let's pray that prayer to Gabriel, to Saint Bernard, to D.L. Moody. Let's pray that prayer to any man or creature that has ever served God. You can't pray that kind of prayer to a creature. To put those word into a hymn means that the one about whom you are speaking must be God.

Holy Ghost, with power divine,
Cleanse this guilty heart of mine.

Who can get into the intricate depths of a human soul, into the deep confines of a human spirit and cleanse it? Nobody but the God who made it! The hymn writer who said "Cleanse this guilty heart of mine" meant that the Holy Ghost to whom he prayed was God.

Holy Spirit, all divine,
Dwell within this heart of mine;
Cast down every idol throne;
Reign supreme—and reign alone.

The church has sung that now for about one hundred years. *"Reign supreme—and reign alone."* Could you pray that to anybody you know? The man who wrote that hymn believed that the Holy Ghost was God, otherwise he wouldn't have said, "Reign supreme, and reign all by Yourself." That is an invitation no man can make to anybody, except the Divine One, except God.

What the Scriptures say

Now the Scriptures. Notice that I am trying to establish the truth that the Holy Spirit is not only a Person, but that He is a divine Person; not only a divine Person, but God.

In Psalm 139 the hymnist attributes omnipresence to the Holy Ghost. He says, "Whither shall I go from thy spirit? or whither shall I flee from thy presence?" (139:7) and he develops throughout the 139th Psalm, in language that is as beautiful as a sunrise and as musical as the wind through the willows, the idea that the Spirit is everywhere, having the attributes of deity. He must be deity, for no creature could have the attributes of deity.

In Hebrews there is attributed to the Holy Ghost that which is never attributed to an archangel, or a seraphim, or a cherubim, or an angel, or an apostle, or a martyr,

or a prophet, or a patriarch, or anyone that
has ever been created by the hand of God.
It says, "through the eternal Spirit" (Hebrews 9:14), and every theologian knows
that eternity is an attribute of no creature
which deity has ever formed. The angels
are not eternal; that is, they had a beginning, and all created things had a beginning. As soon as the word "eternal" is used
about being it immediately establishes the
fact that he never had a beginning, is not a
creature at all, but God. Therefore, when
the Holy Ghost says "the eternal Spirit"
about Himself He is calling Himself God.

Again, the baptismal formula in Matthew 28:19 says, "baptizing them in the
name of the Father, and of the Son, and of
the Holy Ghost." Now try to imagine putting the name of a man in there: "baptizing
them in the name of the Father, and of the
Son, and of the Apostle Paul." You couldn't
think it! It is horrible to contemplate! No
man can be admitted into that closed circle
of deity. We baptize in the name of the Father and the Son, because in the Son is
equal with the Father in His Godhead, and
we baptize in the name of the Holy Ghost

because the Holy Ghost is also equal with
the Father and the Son.

You say, "You are just a Trinitarian and
we are Trinitarians already." Yes, I know it,
but once again I tell you that I am trying to
throw emphasis upon this teaching.

How many blessed truths have gotten
snowed under. People believe them, but
they are just not being taught, that is all.
Here was a man and his wife, a very fine in-
telligent couple from another city. They
named the church to which they belonged,
and I instantly said, "That is a fine church!"

"Oh, yes," they said, "but they don't
teach what we came over here for." They
came over because they were ill and
wanted to be scripturally anointed for healing. So I got together two missionaries, two
preachers and an elder, and we anointed
them and prayed for them. If you were to
go to that church where they attended and
say to the preacher, "Do you believe that
the Lord answers prayer and heals the
sick?" he would reply, "Sure, I do!" He believes it, but he doesn't teach it, and what
you don't believe strongly enough to teach
doesn't do you any good.

It is the same with the fullness of the Holy Ghost. Evangelical Christianity believes it, but nobody experiences it. It lies under the snow, forgotten. I am praying that God may be able to melt away the ice from this blessed truth, and let it spring up alive again, that the Church and the people who hear may get some good out of it and not merely say, "I believe" while it is buried under the snow of inactivity and non-attention.

Let us recapitulate. Who is the Spirit? The Spirit is God, existing in another mode of being than ourselves. He exists as a spirit and not as matter, for He is not matter, but He is God. He is a Person. It was so believed by the whole Church of Christ down through the years. It was so sung by the hymnists back in the days of the first hymn writers. It is so taught in the Book, all through the Old Testament and the New, and I have given you only a few proof texts. I could spend the evening reading Scripture stating this same thing.

What Is He Like?

Now what follows from all this? Ah, there is an unseen Deity present, a knowing, feeling Personality, and He is indivisible from the Father and the Son, so that if you were to be suddenly transferred to heaven itself you wouldn't be any closer to God than you are now, for God is already here. Changing your geographical location would not bring you any nearer to God nor God any nearer to you, because the indivisible Trinity is present, and all that the Son is the Holy Ghost is, and all that the Father is the Holy Ghost is, and the Holy Ghost is in His Church.

What will we find Him to be like? He will be exactly like Jesus. You have read your New Testament, and you know what Jesus is like, and the Holy Spirit is exactly like Jesus, for Jesus was God and the Spirit is God, and the Father is exactly like the Son; and you can know what Jesus is like by knowing what the Father is like, and you can know what the Spirit is like by knowing what Jesus is like.

If Jesus were to come walking down this aisle there would be no stampede for the door. Nobody would scream and be frightened. We might begin to weep for sheer joy and delight that He had so honored us, but nobody would be afraid of Jesus; no mother with a little crying babe would ever have to be afraid of Jesus; no poor harlot being dragged by the hair of her head had to be afraid of Jesus—nobody! Nobody ever had to be afraid of Jesus, because He is the epitome of love, kindliness, geniality, warm attractiveness and sweetness. And that is exactly what the Holy Ghost is, for He is the Spirit of the Father and the Son. *Amen.*

CHAPTER TWO

THE PROMISE
OF THE FATHER

*And, behold, I send the promise of my Father
upon you: but tarry ye in the city of Jerusalem,
until ye be endued with power from on high.
(Luke 24:49)*

I wonder if you have ever thought of the origin of the phrase Jesus used here. Why did He call it the Father's promise? He didn't say "mine." He said, "The promise of my Father." This takes us back to Joel 2:28-29:

And it shall come to pass afterward, that I will pour out my spirit upon all flesh; and your sons and your daughters shall prophesy, your old men shall dream dreams, your young men shall see visions: and also upon the servants and upon the handmaids in those days will I pour out my spirit.

15

Now, when our Lord Jesus came He authoritatively interpreted this, and tied up His intention for His Church with the ancient promises given by the Father centuries before.

In fulfillment of all this there were three periods discernible in the New Testament: (1) The period of the promise, (2) the period of the preparation and (3) the period of the realization—all this having to do with the promise of the Father and the intention of the Son toward His people.

The Period of the Promise

The period of the promise extends from John the Baptist, roughly, to the resurrection of our Lord Jesus. The marks of it are these: that there were disciples, and they were commissioned and instructed, and they exercised their commission and the authority granted them by the Lord. They knew the Lord Jesus; they loved Him. They knew Him living, they knew Him and saw Him dead, and they saw Him risen again from the dead. All the time our Lord was with them. *He was busy creating expectation in them.* He was telling His disciples that in spite of all they had and all the blessing that

God the Father had given them, they were still to expect the coming of a new and superior kind of life. He was creating an expectation of an effusion of outpoured energy which they, at their best, did not yet enjoy.

The Period of the Preparation

Then our Lord rose from the dead and we have what we call the period of the preparation. That was the short period of the preparation. That was the short period which intervened between our Lord's resurrection and the down-coming of the Holy Ghost. They had stopped their activity at the specific command of the Lord. He said, "Tarry! You are about to receive that which has been promised. Your expectations are about to be fulfilled, your hopes realized. Therefore, don't do anything until it comes."

I might say here that sometimes you are going farther when you are not going anywhere; you are moving faster when you are not moving at all; you are learning more when you think you have stopped learning. These disciples had reached an impasse. Their Lord had risen, and they had seen Him, and with excitement and joy they knew He had risen from the dead. Now He had gone from them. Where was He? They gathered together, as you and I might have done under like circumstances, waiting, all of one accord. That is more than they had done during the period of the promise. But here were 120 of them, and they had a oneness of accord.

The Period of the Realization

The period of realization came upon them when the Father fulfilled His promise and sent the Spirit. Peter used a phrase to describe it which is one of the fullest, finest phrases I know. He said, "He hath shed forth this, which ye now see and hear" (Acts 2:33)—the shedding forth was like a mighty down-coming of water. The expectations were more than met—not fully met, but more than met. God always gives us an overplus. They got more than they expected.

Now what happened here? What did they receive that they had not had before? Well, first, they had a new kind of evidence for the reality of their faith. You see, Christ talked about four lines of evidence of His Messiahship.

He said, "Search the scriptures; for in them ye think ye have eternal life: and they are they which testify of me" (John 5:39). The Scriptures were proof of who Christ was. That is one line of evidence.

Another line is the witness of John the Baptist who pointed to Jesus and said, "Behold the Lamb of God, which taketh away the sin of the world" (1:29).

Jesus gives us another line of evidence. He said, "The Father himself . . . hath borne witness of me" (5:37), and there was a third proof of His Messiahship, and authentic proof of it.

He gave a fourth. He said, "The same works that I do, bear witness of me, that the Father hath sent me. . . . Believe me for the very works' sake" (5:36; 14:11).

Have you noticed there is one serious breakdown there, a breakdown which our Lord recognized and which He remedied when the Holy Spirit came? That breakdown lies in the necessary externality of the proof. In every instance the proofs which our Lord adduced to His own Messiahship were external to the individual. They are not inside of the man. He has to open the Book and read. That is external to the man.

When I hear that the Church of Christ has gone throughout the whole world carrying the torch of civilization, healing and giving hope and help, I conclude the Christian Church must be of God because she is acting the way God would act. When I hear that she has founded hospitals and insane asylums, I say surely she must be of God because that is what God would do, being what He is. When I hear that she has emancipated woman and has taken her from being a chattel slave and an object of some old king's lust to being the equal of the man and queen in his home, I say surely that must be of God.

You can go down the corridors of history, and you can adduce proof of the divinity of the Church from what the Church has done. You can show how she brought civilization here and she brought help there. She cleaned up saloons in this town, and she delivered this young fellow from drink. We say that must be God. But that is external proof and it depends upon logic.

A.W. Tozer

The Internal Evidence

There is another kind of evidence. *It is the immediate evidence of the inner life.* That is the evidence by which you know you are alive. If I were to prove that you weren't alive, you would chuckle and go home just as alive as you are now and not be a bit worried about it, because you have the instant, unmediated evidence of internal life.

Jesus Christ wanted to take religion out of the external and make it internal and put it on the same level as life itself, so that a man knows he knows God the same as he knows he is himself and not somebody else. He knows he knows God the same as he knows he is alive and not dead. Only the Holy Ghost can do that. The Holy Spirit came to carry the evidence of Christianity from the books of apologetics into the human heart, and that is exactly what He does.

You can take the gospel of Jesus Christ to the heathen in Borneo, or Africa, people who could never conceive the first premise of your logical arguments, so that it would be totally impossible for them to decide on logical grounds whether Christianity was of God or not. Preach Christ to them and

21

they will believe and be transformed and put away their wickedness and change from evil to righteousness and get happy about it all, learn to read and write and study their Bibles and become leaders and pillars in their own church, transformed and made over. How? By the instant witness of the Holy Ghost to their hearts. This is the new thing that came, sir! God took religion from the realm of the external and made it internal.

Our trouble is that we are trying to confirm the truth of Christianity by an appeal to external evidence. We are saying, "Well, look at this fellow. He can throw a baseball farther than anybody else and he is a Christian, therefore Christianity must be true." "Here is a great statesman who believes the Bible. Therefore, the Bible must be true." We quote Daniel Webster or Roger Bacon. We write books to show that some scientist believed in Christianity: therefore, Christianity must be true.

We are all the way out on the wrong track, brother! That is not New Testament Christianity at all. That is a pitiful, whimpering, drooling appeal to the flesh. That never was the testimony of the New Testa-

ment, never the way God did things—
never! You might satisfy the intellects of
men by external evidences, and Christ did,
I say, point to external evidence when He
was here on earth.

The Witness of the Holy Spirit

But He said, "I am sending you something better. I am taking Christian
apologetics out of the realm of logic and
putting it into the realm of life. I am prov-
ing My deity, and My proof will not be an
appeal to a general or a prime minister. The
proof lies in an invisible, unseen but pow-
erful energy that visits the human soul
when the gospel is preached—the Holy
Ghost!"

The Spirit of the living God brought an
evidence that needed no logic; it went
straight to the soul like a flash of silver light,
like the direct plunge of a sharp spear into
the heart. Those are the very words that
Scripture uses when it says "pierced
(pricked) to the heart." One translator
points out that that word "pricked" is a
word that means that it goes in deeper than
the spear that pierced Jesus' side!

That is the way God does. There is an immediate witness, an unmeditated push of the Spirit of God upon the spirit of man. There is a filtering down, a getting down into the very cells of that human soul and the impression on that soul by the Holy Ghost that this is true. That is what those disciples had never had before, and that is exactly what the Church does not have now. That is what we fundamentalist preachers wish we had and don't have, and that is why we are going so far astray to prove things. That, incidentally, is why this humble pulpit is never open to a man who wants to prove Christianity by means of appeal to external evidence. You can't do it to begin with, and I wouldn't do it to end with. We have something better.

Then, also, the Spirit gave a bright, emotional quality to their religion, and I grieve before my God over the lack of this in our day. The emotional quality isn't there. There is a sickliness about us all; we pump so hard trying to get a little drop of delight out of our old rusty well, and we write innumerable bouncy choruses, and we pump and pump until you could hear the old rusty thing squeak across forty acres. But it doesn't work.

Then He gave them direct spiritual authority. By that I mean He removed their fears, their questions, their apologies and their doubts, and they had an authority that was founded upon life.

The Spirit Comes Today

There is a great modern error which I want to mention: it is that the coming of the Spirit happened once and for all, that the individual Christian is not affected by it. It is like the birth of Christ which happened once and for all and the most excellent sermon on the birth of Christ would never have that birth repeated, and all the prayers in the wide world would never have Christ born again of the Virgin Mary.

It is, they say, like the death and resurrection of Christ—never to be repeated. This error asserts that the coming of the Holy Spirit is an historic thing, an advance in the dispensational workings of God; but that it is all settled now and we need give no further thought to it. It is all here and we have it all, and if we believe in Christ that is it and there isn't anything more.

All right. Now everybody has a right to his view, if he thinks it is scriptural; but I would just like to ask some questions. I won't answer them; I'll just ask them, and you preach your own sermon.

Is the promise of the Father, with all its attendant riches of spiritual grace and power, intended to be for the first-century Christians only? Does the new birth, which the first-century Christians had to have, suffice for all other Christians, or is the new birth which they had to have that which we have to have? Does the new birth have to be repeated in each Christian before it is valid, or did that first church get born again for us? Can you get born again by proxy? The fact that those first 120 were born again, does that mean that we don't have to be? Now you answer me.

You say, "No, certainly we agree that everybody has to have the new birth for himself, individually." All right, if that is true (and it is), is the fullness of the Spirit which those first Christians received enough? Does that work for you and me? They had the fullness; now they are dead. Does the fact that they were filled avail to me? You answer that question.

Again, I want to ask you, would a meal eaten by Saint Peter in the year A.D. 33

nourish me today? Would a good meal of barley cakes and milk, and honey spread on the barley cake—a good meal for a good Jew in Peter's day—nourish me today? No, Peter is dead, and I can't be nourished by what Peter ate.

Would the fullness of the Holy Ghost that Peter got in the upper chamber do for me today, or must I receive individually what Peter received?

What value would the fullness of the Spirit in the church in Jerusalem have for us today if it was done over there once for all and we can't have the same thing here? We are separated by 5,000 miles of water and by 2,000 years of time. Now what, that happened to them, can possibly avail to us?

I want to ask you some more questions: Do you see any similarity between the average one of us Christians buzzing around Chicago and those apostles? Are you ready to believe that we have just what they had, and that every believer in Chicago who accepts the Bible and is converted immediately enters into and now enjoys and possesses exactly what they did back there? Surely you know better than that!

This modern fundamentalism as we know it and of which we are a part—is it a satisfactory fulfillment of the expectations raised by the Father and Christ? Our Father who is in heaven raised certain high expectations of what He was going to do for His redeemed people. When His Son came to redeem those people, He heightened those expectations, raised them, clarified them, extended them, enlarged them and emphasized them. He raised an expectation that was simply beyond words, too wonderful and beautiful and thrilling to imagine. I want to ask you: Is this level of Christianity which we fundamentalists in this city now enjoy what He meant by what He said?

Listen, brother. Our Lord Jesus Christ advertised that He was going away to the Father and He was going to send back for His people a wonderful gift, and He said, "Stay right here until it comes, because it will be the difference between failure and success to you."

Then the Spirit came. Was He equal to the advertising? Did they say, "*Is this* all He meant! Oh, it is disappointing!" No. The Scripture says they wondered. The word "wonder" is in their mouths and hearts. He gave so much more than He promised, because words were the promise and the Holy Ghost was the fulfillment.

The simple fact is that we believers are not up to what He gave us reason to expect. The only honest thing to do is admit this and do something about it. There certainly has been a vast breakdown somewhere between promise and fulfillment. That breakdown is not with our heavenly Father, for He always gives more than He promises.

Now I am going to ask that you reverently ponder this and set aside time and search the Scriptures, pray and yield, obey and believe, and see whether that which our Lord gave us reason to think could be the possession of the Church may not be ours in actual fulfillment and realization.

CHAPTER THREE

HOW TO BE FILLED WITH THE HOLY SPIRIT

Before we deal with the question of how to be filled with the Holy Spirit, there are some matters which first have to be settled. As believers you have to get them out of the way, and right here is where the difficulty arises. I have been afraid that my listeners might have gotten the idea somewhere that I had a how-to-be-filled-with-the-Spirit-in-five-easy-lessons doctrine, which I could give you. If you can have any such vague ideas as that, I can only stand before you and say, "I am sorry"; because it isn't true; I can't give you such a course. There are some things, I say, that you have to get out of the way, settled. One of them is: Before you are filled with the Holy Spirit you must *be sure that you can be filled*.

Is the Spirit-Filled Life for You?

Satan has opposed the doctrine of the Spirit-filled life about as bitterly as any other doctrine there is. He has confused it, opposed it, surrounded it with false notions and fears. He has blocked every effort of the Church of Christ to receive from the Father her divine and blood-bought patrimony. The Church has tragically neglected this great liberating truth—that there is now for the child of God a full and wonderful and completely satisfying anointing with the Holy Ghost.

So you have to be sure that it is for you. You must be sure that it is God's will for you; that is, that it is part of the total plan, that it is included and embraced within the work of Christ in redemption; that it is, as the old camp-meeting, praying folks used to say, "the purchase of His blood."

I might throw a bracket in here and say that whenever I use the neutral pronoun "it" I am talking about the gift. When I speak directly of the Holy Spirit, I shall use a personal pronoun, *He* or *Him* or *His*, referring to a person, for the Holy Spirit is not an *it*, but the *gift* of the Holy Spirit must necessarily in our English language be called "it."

Can you believe this is part of God's plan?

You must, I say, be satisfied that this is nothing added or extra. The Spirit-filled life is not a special, deluxe edition of Christianity. It is part and parcel of the total plan of God for His people.

You must be satisfied that it is not abnormal. I admit that it is unusual, because there are so few people who walk in the light of it or enjoy it, but it is not abnormal. In a world where everybody was sick, health would be unusual, but it wouldn't be abnormal. This is unusual only because our spiritual lives are so wretchedly sick and so far down from where they should be.

Can you believe the Spirit is lovable?

You must be satisfied, again, that there is nothing about the Holy Spirit queer or strange or eerie. I believe it has been the work of the devil to surround the person of the Holy Spirit with an aura of queerness, or strangeness, so that the people of God feel that this Spirit-filled life is a life of being odd and peculiar, of being a bit uncanny.

That is not true, my friend! The devil manufactured that. He hatched it out, the same devil that once said to our ancient mother, "Yea, hath God said," and thus maligned God Almighty. That same devil has maligned the Holy Ghost. There is nothing eerie, nothing queer, nothing contrary to the normal operations of the human heart about the Holy Ghost. He is only the essence of Jesus imparted to believers. You read the four Gospels and see for yourself how wonderfully calm, pure, sane, simple, sweet, natural and lovable Jesus was. Even philosophers who don't believe in His deity have to admit the lovableness of His character.

You must be sure of all this to the point of conviction. That is, you must be convinced to a point where you won't try to persuade God.

You don't have to persuade God at all. There is no persuasion necessary. Dr. A.B. Simpson used to say, "Being filled with the Spirit is as easy as breathing; you can simply breathe out and breathe in." He wrote a hymn to that effect. I am sorry that it is not a better hymn, because it is wonderful theology.

Can you believe this is scriptural?

Unless you have arrived at this place in your listening and thinking and meditating and praying, where you know that the Spirit-filled life is for you, that there is no doubt about it—no book you read or sermon you heard, or tract somebody sent you is bothering you; you are restful about all this; you are convinced that in the blood of Jesus when He died on the cross there was included, as a purchase of that blood, your right to a full, Spirit-filled life—unless you are convinced of that, unless you are convinced that it isn't an added, unusual, extra, deluxe something that you have to go to God and beg and beat your fists on the chair to get, I recommend this to you: I recommend that you don't do anything about it yet except to meditate upon the Scriptures bearing on this truth.

Go to the Word of God and to those parts of it which deal with the subject under discussion tonight and meditate upon them; for "faith cometh by hearing, and hearing by the word of God" (Romans 10:17). Real faith springs not out of sermons but out of the Word of God and out of sermons only so far as they are of the Word of God. I recommend that you be calm and confident about this. Don't get excited, don't despond. The darkest hour is just before the dawn. It may be that this moment of discouragement which you are going through is preliminary to a sunburst of new and beautiful living, if you will follow on to know the Lord.

Remember, fear is of the flesh and panic is of the devil. Never fear and never get panicky. When they came to Jesus nobody except a hypocrite ever needed to fear Him. When a hypocrite came to Jesus He just sliced him to bits and sent him away bleeding from every pore. If they were ready to give up their sin and follow the Lord and they came in simplicity of heart and said, "Lord, what do You want me to do?" the Lord took all the time in the world to talk to them and explain to them and to correct any false impressions or wrong ideas they had. He is the sweetest, most understanding and wonderful Teacher in the world, and He never panics anybody. It is sin that does that. If there is a sense of panic upon your life, it may be because there is sin in that life of yours which you need to get rid of.

Do You Want to Be Filled?

Again, before you can be filled with the Spirit you must desire to be filled. Here I meet with a certain amount of puzzlement. Somebody will say, "How is it that you say to us that we must desire to be? Haven't we called you on the phone? Aren't we out here tonight to hear the sermon on the Holy Spirit? Isn't this all a comforting indication to you that we are desirous of being filled with the Holy Spirit?"

Not necessarily, and I will explain why. For instance, are you sure that you want to be possessed by a spirit other than your own? even though that spirit be the pure Spirit of God? even though He be the very gentle essence of the gentle Jesus? even though He be sane and pure and free? even though He be wisdom personified, wisdom Himself, even though He have a healing, precious ointment to distill? even though He be loving as the heart of God? That Spirit, if He ever possess you, will be the Lord of your life!

How to Be Filled with the Holy Spirit
Do you want Him to be Lord of your life?

I ask you, Do you want Him to be Lord of you life? That you want His benefits, I know. I take that for granted. But do you want to be possessed by Him? Do you want to hand the keys of your soul over to the Holy Spirit and say, "Lord, from now on I don't even have a key to my own house. I come and go as Thou tellest me"? Are you willing to give the office of your business establishment, your soul, over to the Lord and say to Jesus, "You sit in this chair and handle these telephones and boss the staff and be Lord of this outfit"? That is what I mean. Are you sure you want to do this? Are you sure that you desire it?

Are you sure that you want your personality to be taken over by One who will expect obedience to the written and living Word? Are you sure that you want your personality to be taken over by One who will not tolerate the self sins? For instance, self-love. You can no more have the Holy Ghost and have self-love than you can have purity and impurity at the same moment in the same place. He will not permit you to indulge self-confidence. Self-love, self-confidence, self-righteousness, self-admiration, self-aggrandizement and self-pity are under the interdiction of God Almighty, and He cannot send His mighty Spirit to possess the heart where these things are.

Again, I ask you if you desire to have your personality taken over by One who stands in sharp opposition to the world's easy ways. No tolerance of evil, no smiling at crooked jokes, no laughing off things that God hates. The Spirit of God, if He takes over, will bring you into opposition to the world just as Jesus was brought into opposition to it. The world crucified Jesus because they couldn't stand Him!

There was something in Him that rebuked them and they hated Him for it and finally crucified Him. The world hates the Holy Ghost as bad as they ever hated Jesus, the One from whom He proceeds. Are you sure, brother? You want His help, yes; you want a lot of His benefits, yes; but are you willing to go with Him in His opposition to the easygoing ways of the world? If you are not, you needn't apply for anything more than you have, because you don't want Him; you only think you do!

Again, are you sure that you need to be filled? Can't you get along the way you are? You have been doing fairly well: You pray, you read your Bible, you give to missions, you enjoy singing hymns, you thank God you don't drink or gamble or attend movie theaters, that you are honest, that you have prayer at home. You are glad about all this. Can't you get along like that? Are you sure you need any more than that?

I want to be fair with you. I want to do what Jesus did: He turned around to them when they were following Him and told them the truth. I don't want to take you in under false pretense. "Are you sure you want to follow Me?" He asked, and a great many turned away. But Peter said, "Lord, to whom shall we go? thou hast the words of eternal life" (John 6:68). And the crowd that wouldn't turn away was the crowd that made history. The crowd that wouldn't turn back was the crowd that was there when the Holy Ghost came and filled all the place where they were sitting. The crowd that turned back never knew what it was all about.

But maybe you feel in your heart that you just can't go on as you are, that the level of spirituality to which you know yourself called is way beyond you. If you feel that there is something that you must have or your heart will never be satisfied, that there are levels of spirituality, mystic deeps and heights of spiritual communion, purity and power that you have never known, that there is fruit which you know you should bear and do not, victory which you know you should have and have not—I would say, "Come on," because God has something for you tonight.

There is a spiritual loneliness, an inner aloneness, an inner place where God brings the seeker, where he is as lonely as if there were not another member of the Church anywhere in the world. Ah, when you come there, there is a darkness of mind, an emptiness of heart, a loneliness of soul, but it is preliminary to the daybreak. *O God, bring us, somehow, to the daybreak!*

How to Receive Him

Here is how to receive. First, *present your body to Him* (Romans 12:1-2). God can't fill what He can't have. Now I ask you: Are

41

you ready to present your body with all of its functions and all that it contains—your mind, your personality, your spirit, your love, your ambitions, your all? That is the first thing. That is a simple, easy act—presenting your body. Are you willing to do it?

Now the second thing is to *ask* (Luke 11:9-13), and I set aside all theological objections to this text. They say that is not for today. Well, why did the Lord leave it in the Bible then? Why didn't He put it somewhere else? Why did He put it where I could see it if He didn't want me to believe it? It is all for us, and if the Lord wanted us to do it, He could give it without our asking, but He chooses to have us ask. "Ask of me, and I shall give thee" (Psalm 2:8) is always God's order; so why not ask?

Acts 5:32 tells us the third thing to do. God gives His Holy Spirit to them that *obey* Him. Are you ready to obey and do what you are asked to do? What would that be? Simply to live by the Scriptures as you understand them. Simple, but revolutionary.

The next thing is, *have faith* (Galatians 3:2). We receive Him by faith as we receive the Lord in salvation by faith. He comes as a gift of God to us in power. First He comes

42

in some degree and measure when we are converted, otherwise we couldn't be converted. Without Him we couldn't be born again, because we are born of the Spirit. But I am talking about something different now, an advance over that. I am talking about His coming and possessing the full body and mind and life and heart, taking the whole personality over, gently, but directly and bluntly, and making it His, so that we may become a habitation of God through the Spirit.

So now suppose we sing. Let us sing "The Comforter Has Come," because He has come. If He hasn't come to your heart in fullness, He will; but He has come to earth. He is here and ready, when we present our vessel, to fill our vessel if we will ask and believe. Will you do it?

CHAPTER FOUR

HOW TO CULTIVATE THE SPIRIT'S COMPANIONSHIP

Can two walk together, except they be agreed?
(Amos 3:3)

Now this is what is known as a rhetorical question; it is equivalent to a positive declaration that two cannot walk together except they be agreed, and for two to walk together they must be in some sense one.

They also have to agree that they *want* to walk together, and they have to agree that it is to their advantage to travel together. I think you will see that it all adds up to this: *For two to walk together voluntarily they must be, in some sense, one.*

I am talking now about how we can cultivate the Spirit's fellowship, how we can walk with Him day by day and hour by hour—and you won't object if I say "you." (Sometimes we preachers preach in the third person, and you can develop a habit of thinking in the third person. We don't talk about "us"; we talk about "they." I don't like that. I think we ought to get personal about this.)

Are You Ready for This?

There are some of you who are not ready for this sermon at all. You are trying to face both ways at once. You are trying to take some of this world and to get some of that world over yonder. You are a Christian, but I am talking about an advance upon the first early stages of salvation and the cultivation of the presence of the Holy Ghost, so that He may illuminate and bless and lift and purify and direct your life. You are not ready for this, because you haven't given up all that you might have the All. You want some, but you don't want all; that is the reason you are not ready.

You who have not given up the world will not be able to understand what I am talking about. You want Christianity for its insurance value. You want just what a man wants when he takes out policy on his life, or his car or his house. You don't want modernism, because it hasn't any insurance value. You are willing to support this proposition financially. He would be a poor man who would want insurance and not be willing to pay for it. If Jesus Christ died for you on the cross you are very happy about that because it means you won't be brought into judgment, but have passed from death into life. You are willing to live reasonably well, because that is the premium you are paying for the guarantee that God will bless you while you live and take you home to heaven when you die!

You may not be ready because your conception of religion is social and not spiritual. There are people like that. They have watered down the religion of the New Testament until it has no strength in it. They have introduced the water of their own opinion into it until it has no taste left. They are socially minded. This is as far as it goes with them. People like that they may be saved. I am not prepared to say that they are not saved, but I am prepared to say that they are not ready for what I am talking about. The gospel of Christ is essentially spiritual, and Christian truth working upon human souls by the Holy Ghost makes Christian men and women spiritual.

I don't want to say this, but I think that some of you may not be ready for this message because you are more influenced by the world than you are by the New Testament. I am perfectly certain that I could rake up fifteen boxcar loads of fundamentalist Christians this hour in the city of Chicago who are more influenced in their whole outlook by Hollywood than they are by the Lord Jesus Christ. I am positive that much that passes for the gospel in our day is very little more than a very mild case of orthodox religion grafted on to a heart that is sold out to the world in its pleasures and tastes and ambitions.

The kind of teaching that I have been giving has disturbed some people. I am not going to apologize at all, because, necessarily, if I have been traveling along thinking I am all right and there comes a man of God and tells me that there is yet much land to be possessed, it will disturb me. That is the preliminary twinge that comes to the soul that wants to know God. Whenever the Word of God hits us, it disturbs us. So don't be disturbed by the disturbance. Remember that it is quite normal. God has to jar us loose.

But there are some who are prepared. They are those who have made the grand, sweet committal. They have seen heaven draw nearer and earth recede; the things of this world have become less and less attractive, and the things of heaven have begun to pull and pull as the moon pulls at the sea, and they are prepared now. So I am going to give you these few little pointers to help you into a better life.

1. The Holy Spirit Is a Living Person

The Holy Spirit is the third Person of the Trinity. He is Himself God, and as a Person, He can be cultivated; He can be wooed and cultivated the same as any person can be. People grow on us, and the Holy Spirit, being a Person, can grow on us.

2. Be Engrossed with Jesus Christ

Be engrossed with and honor Jesus Christ. John said: "But this spake he of the Spirit, which they that believe on him should receive: for the Holy Ghost was not yet given; because that Jesus was not yet glorified" (John 7:39).

I ask you to note that the Spirit was given when Jesus was glorified. Now that is a principle. Remember that He came and spread Himself out as a flood upon the people because Jesus was glorified. He established a principle, and He will never, never flood the life of any man except the man in whom Jesus is glorified. Therefore, if you dedicate yourself to the glory of Jesus, the Holy Ghost will become the aggressor and will seek to know you and raise you and illumine you and fill you and bless you. Honoring Jesus Christ is doing the things which Jesus told you to do, trusting Him as your All, following Him as your Shepherd, and obeying Him fully.

Let's cultivate the Holy Ghost by honoring the Lord Jesus. As we honor Jesus, the Spirit of God becomes glad within us. He ceases to hold back, He relaxes and becomes intimate and communes and imparts Himself; and the sun comes up and heaven comes near as Jesus Christ becomes our all in all.

To glorify Jesus is the business of the Church, and to glorify Jesus is the work of the Holy Ghost. I can walk with Him when I am doing the same things He is doing, and go the same way He is going and travel at the same speed He is traveling. I must be engrossed with Jesus Christ. I must honor Him. "If any man serve me, him will my Father honour" (John 12:26). So let's honor the Lord Jesus. Not only theologically, but let's honor Him personally.

3. Walk in Righteousness

Let's walk in righteousness. The grace of God that bringeth salvation also teaches the heart that we should deny ungodliness and worldly lusts and live soberly and righteously and godly in this present world. There you have the three dimensions of life. Soberly—that is me. Righteously—that is my fellowman. Godly—that is God. Let us not make the mistake of thinking we can be spiritual and not be good. Let's not make the mistake of thinking we can walk with the Holy Ghost and go a wrong or dirty or an unrighteous way, for how can two walk together except they be agreed? He is the *Holy* Spirit, and if I walk in an unholy way, how can I fellowship with Him?

4. Make Your Thoughts a Clean Sanctuary

To God, our thoughts are things. Our thoughts are the decorations inside the sanctuary where we live. If our thoughts are purified by the blood of Christ, we are living in a clean room no matter if we are wearing overalls covered with grease. Your thoughts pretty much decide the mood and weather and climate inside your heart, and God considers your thoughts as part of you.

Thoughts of peace, thoughts of pity, thoughts of charity, thoughts of God, thoughts of the Son of God—these are pure things, good things and high things. Therefore, if you would cultivate the Spirit's acquaintance, you must get hold of your thoughts and not allow your mind to be a wilderness in which every kind of unclean beast roams and bird flies. You must have a clean heart.

5. Seek to Know Him in the Word

It is in the Word we find the Holy Spirit. Don't read too many other things. Some of you will say, "Look who's talking!" Well, go ahead and say it, I don't mind; but I am reading fewer and fewer things as I get older, not because I am losing interest in this great big old suffering world, but because I am gaining interest in that other world above. So I say, don't try to know everything. You can't. Find Him in the Word, for the Holy Ghost wrote this Book. He inspired it, and He will be revealed in its pages.

What is the word when we come to the Bible? It is *meditate*. We are to come to the Bible and meditate. That is what the old saints did. They meditated. They laid the Bible on their old-fashioned handmade chair, got down on the old, scrubbed board floor and meditated on the Word. As they meditated, faith mounted. The Spirit and faith illuminated. They had nothing but a Bible with fine print and narrow margins and poor paper, but they knew their Bible better than some of us with all our helps. Let's practice the art of Bible meditation.

Now please don't grab that phrase book and go out and form a club. Don't do it! Just meditate. That is what we need. We are organized to death already. Let's just be plain Christians. Let's open the Bible, spread it out on the chair, and meditate on it. It will open itself to us, and the Spirit of God will come and brood over it.

So be a meditator. I challenge you: Try it for a month and see how it works. Put away questions and answers and the filling in of blank lines about Noah. Put all that cheap trash away and take a Bible, open it, get on your knees and say, "Father, here I am. Begin to teach me." He will begin to teach you, and He will teach you about Himself and about Jesus and about God and about the Word and about life and death and heaven and hell, and about His own presence.

6. Cultivate the Art of Recognizing the Presence of the Spirit

I have just one more point: Cultivate the art of recognizing the presence of the Spirit everywhere. Get acquainted with the Holy Ghost and then begin to cultivate His presence. When you wake in the morning, in place of burying your head behind the *Tribune*, couldn't you get in just a few thoughts of God while you eat your grapefruit?

Remember, cultivating the Holy Ghost's acquaintance is a job. It is something you do, and yet it is so easy and delightful. It is like cultivating your baby's acquaintance. You know when you first look at the little wrinkled fellow, yelling, all mouth, you don't know him. He is a little stranger to you. Then you begin to cultivate him, and he smiles. (It isn't a smile at all. He has colic! You think it is a smile, and it is such a delight.) Pretty soon he wiggles an arm, and you think he is waving at you. Then he gurgles and you think he said "mama." You get acquainted!

Is this for ministers? Is it for housewives? Yes—housewives and clerks and milkmen and students. If you will thus see it and thus believe it and thus surrender to it, there won't be a secular store in the pavement. There won't be a common, profane deed that you will ever do. The most menial task can become a priestly ministration when the Holy Ghost takes over and Christ becomes your all in all.

Filled with the Spirit . . . Then What?

R. Mabel Francis

FOREWORD

This is an excellent book about what it truly means to be filled with the Holy Spirit.

Mabel Francis has powerfully proven that just an act of being filled with the Holy Spirit does not guarantee continuous victory for the Christian. She shows that there is more to it than that as she clearly reveals the scriptural perspective of steps necessary in our lives for continually abiding in victory.

Miss Francis shows it means dealing with the ugly side of our personality in order to be completely filled with the Spirit. It means Christ in us and not we ourselves—keeping our eyes on Jesus. Then she movingly tells us it means not, petting ourselves, but crucifying ourselves and all the traits of self. We, with Jesus, must die.

One of the most important points she makes is that the Holy Spirit is given to those who *obey* God (see Acts 5:32).

Being filled with the Holy Spirit is not an instant cure-all for all the ills of the Christian life. This book is an honest, biblically accurate, blueprint of the walk in the Holy Spirit. It is a beautifully balanced lifestyle for all of us seeking real victory in Jesus.

Evelyn Christenson
April 1992

CHAPTER ONE

AM I REALLY ANXIOUS FOR A LIFE OF VICTORY?

*I must take the path
"down" that Jesus took!*

On the plane coming home to "retire" after a long and happy ministry to the dear Japanese people, the Lord said to me: "I have a new commission for you. You have followed Me in Japan. Now I want you to tell the people at home what I have taught you."

That was a number of years ago, and although I had thought that I could never leave Japan, I must confess that I have been even happier in my home ministry telling people everywhere of the gracious secrets of spiritual victory over the ugly "self" life within us.

Many of God's dear people have by faith received the fullness of the Holy Spirit, but they still find themselves being impatient, especially in the home.

Many become irritated when they are falsely accused or slandered. They give way to sensitiveness and self-pity.

They begin to wonder: *Why should I have all these difficulties? Didn't I receive the fullness of the Holy Spirit as an act of faith after all?*

Doubt and confusion and discouragement seem to follow these questions. So they go back over their experience with critical evaluation, and many seem to be living under a sense of condemnation as a result.

My own personal testimony about earlier years of my Christian life, and even the earlier years of my missionary service, includes the same kind of struggles and conflicts that perplex many in our churches today.

I knew that I had definitely received the fullness of the Holy Spirit into my life and into my being. So, during many times of testing, I too wondered why the same old conflicts and discouragements would arise within me.

It is right here that many of us make our mistake. The truth is that the Holy Spirit does not make us humanly perfect and does not guarantee that we will automatically spend the rest of our lives on a spiritual mountaintop!

See Self-Life As God Sees It

I think that many Christians honestly do not realize that the Spirit of God wants to show them their own self-life as God sees it. There cannot be full spiritual victory within any individual who is not willing to deal with that ugly life of self, applying God's own prescription of complete identification with the death of Jesus Christ.

The path of death is humbling, but what about the road that Jesus followed? He went straight to the cross. Straight to death!

Jesus humbled Himself and became a man—and I tell you, that was really humbling for the Son of God.

He was the Creator—but He was willing to come to us in the form of the created being. We can never fully know what that meant.

Then He became as a servant, the lowest of men, without even a place to lay His head.

In this humility, He became obedient even unto death, the death of the cross.

And isn't that what our Lord asks of us?

"And whosoever doth not bear his cross, and come after me, cannot be my disciple" (Luke 14:27), said Jesus.

Don't you see that the blessed outcome of His humility, His willingness to take the path "down," His death on the cross, was this: "Wherefore God also hath highly exalted him" (Philippians 2:9)—our Lord Jesus Christ is on the highest seat that anyone could ever take.

He is in the glory! He lives! He is there ruling and reigning!

The only way that we can know His victory and His glory is just to let Him come in His fullness and take over. If we do not acknowledge this secret as the means of dealing with sin and self, we will never experience the gracious fulfillment of our being made one with Him, our nature fused in oneness with the divine nature of our Victor, Jesus Christ.

We receive the fullness of the Holy Spirit by faith. He comes into our hearts and we know that He has come. He comes to teach us of Christ and He wants to show us what we are in terms of our old self-life. He wants to show us so Christ can take over the reins, and He will keep knocking at any little door in your life that you have closed off for yourself!

CHAPTER TWO

DO I HOLD THE
IDEA THAT I AM
COMPLETE IN MYSELF?

*Jesus wants to become
my "Completeness"!*

Many people receive the fullness of the Holy Spirit with marvelous blessing and victory—and then, because of failure to keep their eyes on Jesus as their over-coming portion, they have found everything around them gray and dim once more!

What was that water—that "supply"—that Jesus promised to the woman at the well in the Gospel of John?

Jesus was really saying to her, "I will give you Myself!"

He did not promise that she would have an experience that would keep her from "thirsting" again. Any Christian who believes that that results in continuing spiritual victory will soon be floundering again.

The Scriptures tell us plainly that we must get our eyes away from human experience and feeling. Then, looking only to our Lord Jesus Christ, His Spirit and His victory become a spring bubbling up into everlasting life!

Where is the problem, then?

Looking at Themselves

Instead of looking at the mighty resurrection power of the Lord Jesus, people go back to looking at themselves—and that's why they lose hope and give in so easily to defeat and discouragement.

We are actually dealing here with Christ's supernatural power—not with just our human hopes and resolutions!

How can I be so sure of this kind of divine supply? In Ephesians 3:16, I read this proof:

> May He grant you out of the rich treasury of His glory to be strengthened and reinforced with mighty power in the inner man by the [Holy] Spirit

R. Mabel Francis

[Himself]—indwelling your inner-
most being and personality. (Amp)

He will strengthen and reinforce.

We are right up against the awful conflict
of the ages and no ordinary power will
avail. However, we may be reinforced
within by the Holy Spirit's indwelling our
inner being and personality. This is possible because Christ, the living Christ, dwells
with us and makes His permanent home in
our hearts.

This is the reason for my great joy. Oh,
what a glorious privilege to be able to tell
God's people of the wonderful years of blessing I have known since I found the secret of
letting God take over. This is a moment-
by-moment experience of reckoning and
faith.

Even when we are weak and fail so often,
He has promised that when He is allowed
to come in and take over, it is the fulfillment of our being made one with Him!

I have often thought that it is very much
like the "gold-filled" process that we hear
about in the jewelry trade.

I have a gold-filled watch—but it is not
solid gold! The men in that craft heat up

their little furnaces. They melt a certain amount of gold and they also melt a supply of iron—and then they fuse the two elements together.

My watch is not just gold-plated, it is gold-filled. The gold is fused with the iron and it will never wear off. You see, it is just as nice as if it were all gold. The two metals are fused together and they become one in substance.

Can you see, as I do, that this is a picture of our going on with God in the trials and conflicts and discouragements of life until we get melted down and reckon ourselves to have died with Christ—and so we get fused in with the Person and the nature of our Lord Jesus Christ.

This becomes the secret of His victorious indwelling—you don't know which is which. By faith and by desire and by commitment, we are just one with Him.

Willing to Be Melted Down

But this is what we have to remember—we must be willing to be melted down before we can be fused with Him in His humility and His death and resurrection.

This is the spiritual lesson about which we cannot argue. If we want to have this glorious life of victory, the pathway is down, farther down, all the way down.

But, as we must go down with Him into His death, so it will be with our identification with Him in His resurrection and glory. Colossians 1:27 is actually God's plan for our lives:

> To whom God would make known what is the riches of the glory of this mystery among the Gentiles; which is *Christ in you, the hope of glory.* (emphasis added)

This is our inheritance from God, and I am so anxious for everyone to know this life of victory because it is for us, beloved!

Perhaps it may be with you like it was with me; I found that Jesus Himself wanted to be my "completeness"—and I had been wanting to be complete in myself!

CHAPTER THREE

IS IT GOOD ADVICE
THAT I SHOULD
"CRUCIFY" MYSELF?

*The blessed secret:
"I am crucified with Christ"!*

For many years I quoted the Bible verse, "I am crucified with Christ" (Galatians 2:20), and preached from it too, when it was merely a picture in my mind and I had not come to know the reality of identification with Him in His death. I have heard people say in spiritual counsel: "You must crucify yourself!" But you do not have the power to crucify yourself. More likely you will pet yourself!

Most of us are not willing to admit how very dear "self" is to us. This is where the battle is taking place and this is where we need to acknowledge the work of the Holy Spirit within us.

I am happy to have had the privilege of telling many people in the homeland what God had revealed to me. He showed me that the Holy Spirit had come not only to give me power but also to shed light all through my being so I could recognize the traits of the old self-life.

It was the Holy Spirit who revealed to me that the only way to deal with self in our spiritual life is by death—and death does not come easy!

It was in this light that the Spirit of God revealed to me why the Lord Jesus could not have been slain in a moment. He had to get into the place of death and stay there until death came.

While He was nailed to the cross, the crowd shouted to Him to come down. If He would do this, they said, they would believe that He was the Messiah. But He was drinking a bitter cup and He knew that He had to stay there until He was dead—six long hours!

If we could die immediately in regard to self, it would be much easier!

However, we need time to see all the traits of self and to consign them to the cross one by one—until we have died to all of them. That is what makes it hard.

But how blessed to know now, that instead of going into a spiritual slump when I saw these traits of self, I was to thank God for showing them to me and bring them directly to Him and trust Him to give deliverance at every point.

Bring It to Him

Each time God shows you anything that remains of the old life of self, bring it to Him immediately if you are really concerned about spiritual victory and the overcoming life.

There will always be the inner temptation: "I will deal with it tomorrow!"

Deal with it now. Do not put it aside. Do not excuse it. Let Christ take over in the entire situation, for this assurance of victory and deliverance is possible only when He is allowed to be in control through His Spirit.

This is the kind of Christlike control and direction that people saw in Sophie the Scrubwoman, who was a power for God in the New York Alliance Tabernacle a generation ago.

"I am determined that I am going to have everything that is in the Father's will for me, regardless of what the rest of the heirs say," she would declare. Because she was willing to die out to everything that she might call her own, she bore much fruit for her Savior.

Jesus said that if a kernel of wheat falls into the ground and dies, it brings forth much fruit. We are more likely to think that we can work for Jesus and bring forth fruit by "doing."

But Jesus said: "If it dies"!

I read years ago that an Egyptian mummy entombed for 3,000 years or more was found to have a few grains of wheat in his hand when the wrappings were taken off. Scientists wondered if this wheat would sprout and grow, so the kernels were taken to Canada's great wheat-growing country. They were planted in the proper season and several of the kernels did sprout and grow and reproduce. During the next season these were used as seed again and they reproduced more wheat.

For 3,000 years those grains of wheat were completely dormant; because they were not put into the ground to die, they fed no one. But when they were planted and died, they brought forth fruit and now they are feeding multitudes.

Oh, how much easier it would have been if I had known the secret of death to my old self-life and the blessed secret of spiritual fruit-bearing when I first went to Japan.

I was anxious about many things and, ultimately, the Lord revealed to me that anxiety was sin and hindered His working.

He said to me: "You ask for something and then you proceed to tie My hands by your anxiety." It is His work—and it is my business to believe Him. No strain or stress is necessary. He is over all. It is no longer I, but Christ who dwells within!

Gerhard Tersteegen's hymn expresses this glorious truth:

Is there a thing beneath the sun
    That strives with thee my heart to
        share?
Ah, tear it thence, and reign alone,
    The Lord of every motion there;

Then shall my heart from earth be
free,
When it hath found repose in Thee.

CHAPTER FOUR

DOES GOD DEAL WITH ASPECTS OF THE SELF-LIFE IN CHILDREN?

*Envy and irritation and pride
have no age limits!*

In looking back upon my childhood in New England and my experiences as a Christian girl and young woman, it is very plain to me that I had some personal traits and characteristics with which God had to deal specifically before my life was adequate for service in His great work.

I am going to refer to such attitudes as envy, irritability, disobedience, self-pity, impatience, pride, selfishness, oversensitivity and slowness to forgive.

My life has been peculiarly guided and directed by God. He placed me in a genuine Christian home where devout parents looked always to God in rearing their four daughters and three sons. Regular family prayers and grace at meals gave each of us the foundation for our lives. How thankful I am to God for placing me in such a Christian environment and for making provisions for training me for the work He wanted me to do.

When I was seven years old, Father called my sister, Gertrude, and me to him. He said, "Now, girls, you are old enough to help your mother. Gertrude, I want you to wash the dishes after each meal. Mabel, you are to dry them."

I hated to dry dishes and I found many ways to avoid it. One day after dinner, I complained about a stomachache. Mother said she would dry the dishes in my place. As I saw my tired mother doing my work, I felt greatly condemned. I asked God to help me. He certainly did because after this I did not rebel when it came time to do the work.

Shortly after this, Father was holding a tent meeting and he invited those who were really sorry for their sins to come to the front. I went down the outside aisle to the altar. No one paid any attention to me. I knelt there and asked God's forgiveness for my sins. I also asked God to help me to overcome my hatred of doing housework. After that I tried to live as I felt a Christian should.

Later, Father remarked about my changed disposition, saying, "How happy I am to see such a good helper around the house!"

A Person He Can Use

I had to learn many lessons about how the Lord molds a Christian into a person He can use. I dedicated my life to God, but still I felt something was missing in my life. This troubled me because I could not figure out what my problem could be.

I was really too young at that time to know the full meaning of the word *envy*, but I know that I was troubled about my facial features.

People often remarked about my sister: "Isn't Gertrude beautiful!"

But no one ever said, "Isn't Mabel beautiful!" and this was of great concern to me.

But the Lord did show me that this was really envy, and He dealt with it in my life by giving me an understanding of the great work Queen Esther had done for her people. It was not Esther's beautiful face that counted and made the difference. It was the fact that she was faithful and willing to die that saved her people from death and ruin. It seemed to me that I could envision what would have happened if Esther had failed. She certainly would have heard the cry of her people as they were being slaughtered.

At that point God spoke to me: "If you are not faithful to your call, you will hear the wail of souls going into a Christless eternity." Further, He said: "There is a work for you to do that no one else in all the world can do. There will be a lack in My great plan if you are unfaithful."

During a long illness of my father it was necessary for him to leave home for treatment, and Mother accompanied him. I was placed in charge of my younger brothers and sisters. When they didn't obey my commands, I became vexed and irritable. One night after the children had gone to bed, I went to see if they were all right. I noticed that one brother had been crying; a big tear was standing on his cheek.

I knew that I had caused his crying. I was so convicted that I knelt by his bed and asked God to forgive me. I began to think how kind and thoughtful of others Mother was. I prayed, "Oh God, help me to be more considerate of the feelings of others."

This proved a valuable lesson—a lesson to be learned over and over, not only before I went to Japan but also after I started my work there.

Chapter Five

HOW CAN I SHOW GOD THAT I REALLY WANT TO PLEASE HIM?

*I can love Him completely
instead of loving myself!*

It was not until after I had left home at the age of fifteen to further my education that I learned what the Bible says about the Person and the work of the Holy Spirit. As I read the Word of God, I found that the Holy Spirit is given to those who obey God (Acts 5:32). Now, to me, this meant to obey Him for life. A fierce conflict raged within my heart. How could I say, "Yes, Lord, I will obey," when I did not know what He would ask me to do? I did not understand at the time that He would faithfully lead me step by step!

But first God dealt with me about a very personal matter. He asked me if I were willing to be different from other girls, to give up trying to be outwardly attractive and just to live for Him. I knew then that I should be more simple in my manner of dress and to think less about my personal appearance. I did not have any fine clothes, but I say the desire of my heart was to look pretty and to be admired by my friends.

At that time I wore bangs and spent much time curling them with a hot iron. Whenever it rained the curl would just disappear. This disturbed me and I kept thinking constantly about my appearance. I was distressed when God told me to comb my hair straight back. When I looked in the mirror I thought, *How terrible I look!* I asked the Lord if He really wanted me to look like this. He replied that it looked beautiful to Him. I still hoped that He would change His mind—but He didn't.

God kept asking me, "Do you really want to please Me?" I would answer, "Yes, but . . ." One day I reasoned that if I looked so terrible I would not have a friend on earth. This was such a tremendous battle to me that I became ill and could not meet anyone.

How I praise God for revealing Himself to me through the words of Jesus. "When I was in the Garden of Gethsemane sweating drops of blood for you I was alone (Luke 22:41-44). Aren't you willing to go alone with Me?" This broke my heart, and I said. "Yes, Lord, I am and I will."

Everything Was Different

The blessed Holy Spirit came into my heart in His fullness. Everything seemed changed. There came to me such a burden for people without a knowledge of Christ, people who were *lost,* that I could not rest. Everything was different. The awfulness of a soul being lost was made very real to me.

During my early teaching days I suffered the loss of a very dear friend. How much of my time I spent mourning his loss!

God spoke to me very clearly as I sat by his grave: "You are the only one in this area who knows My love and who has tasted salvation and here you are grieving for this one who you know has gone to heaven." He asked me to put aside this grief and to open a meeting at the school on Sunday afternoons. I was to invite the people to come and then to tell those who came of His salvation. I was startled, but the call was clear and I obeyed. I sent out invitations by the children asking the parents to come.

Before the end of the school year many of those dear country people had found Christ as their personal Savior. The news of these meetings spread to nearby villages. Thus, my Christian ministry was started.

I was nineteen years old and holding evangelistic meetings in Haverhill, Massachusetts, when the Lord spoke clearly to me and gave me a vision of the great nation of Japan. Now I knew where God wanted me to serve—and I was glad!

CHAPTER SIX

WHAT CAN I DO ABOUT A CHRONIC LACK OF PATIENCE?

*I have to confess my failure
and seek the Lord!*

Now that my decision had been made to go to Japan, how anxious I was to get there and start the work of telling the Japanese about my wonderful Savior! But my patience was tested.

First, there was the matter of accumulating funds sufficient for my rail ticket to Seattle, the sea passage to Japan and support for the first year. Also, there were problems of anticipating and collecting my personal effects for life in Japan.

Second, the trip by sea took almost a month and during much of it I was seasick. I felt that I was wasting precious time!

Third, I was an American; therefore, I had to be quarantined on my arrival in Japan. This problem was soon solved, however, for on the second day the American consul, whom I had met on the crossing, requested the authorities to allow me to come to his hotel and take care of his wife, who was ill. While there I was able to find time for prayer and to recover fully from the effects of the long voyage.

Difficulty Communicating

Fourth, how troublesome I found the communication problem! I knew not one word of Japanese and it seemed to take so long to learn just a little. How much time I felt was being lost before I could start my work!

There were no language schools at that time. The only way to learn the language was to sit down and study. A young girl who had just graduated from grammar school came at 9 o'clock every morning and would instruct me in the language until 5 o'clock in the afternoon. When I learned a few words, I would try to put them into a sentence. She would guess what I was trying to say and correct me. If she guessed wrong, I learned wrong. However, she was a bright girl and that helped greatly.

Another thing bothered me and made me impatient: in the early days travel in Japan was very slow. The trains went at the enormous rate of fifteen miles an hour, and everything else seemed just as slow. There were no buses and no cars. (Of course, we didn't have many cars in America then either.) It was often necessary to travel by rickshaw that went only as fast as a man could run. That was not fast enough to suit me! I bought a bicycle so that I could pedal fast and go over the mountains. But, oh, I became so frustrated and so impatient!

Then there were many things about the culture and traditions of the Japanese that I did not understand. I couldn't understand why certain things had to be done in a certain way.

Some of the things the girls did seemed impractical and sometimes even wrong. One girl who helped me was very trying. When washing the stairs she would start from the bottom and walk up on the wet stairs as she washed them. I explained to her that it would be better if she would start at the top and wash down because she would not leave her foot marks on the stairs.

But she would say, "Well, I like my way better," and would continue to do the work her way. It seemed to me that if there were any possible wrong way for her to do a task, she would do it that way.

One morning as I was going to prayer meeting the words of James 1:2 came to me: "Count it all joy when ye fall into divers temptations." The Lord asked me, "Are you considering it all joy about this girl?"

I replied, "No, Lord, I'm considering it very trying."

God Is in All Things

This girl was an orphan and I knew she had nowhere to go if I should dismiss her. However, when I had won the victory over all the little annoyances that came because she always wanted her own way of doing things, she left and God sent me another girl. I began to realize that God was, and is, in all things!

The Japanese attitude toward the time element was also very different from mine. I became annoyed when the girls and my helpers did not appear "on time." One day

I told my girl to have dinner ready at exactly 12 o'clock because I expected a guest. When I came home from a meeting and discovered that the dinner was not ready, I was very perturbed and told her plainly that she had disobeyed me.

But God said to me: "If you had been in the kitchen yourself this morning, you couldn't have done any better. She had one hindrance after another. When things don't go your way, you blame others."

It was so easy for me to blame others when the circumstances were unknown or misunderstood. The Lord was waiting for me to bring this problem to Him. He assures us that His deliverance is always available but only after we have reached the end of our own self-assertion.

CHAPTER SEVEN

WHAT MAKES ME NASTY AND UNPLEASANT TO OTHERS?

*I have not let the Spirit of God
show me my own heart!*

After I began to speak the Japanese language a little better, the mission assigned a Bible woman to help me as a coworker.

One day I said to her, "Now this morning we'll go out to certain places to call."

She replied, "Yes, but just let me go and give the pastor an answer to a question he asked me. It won't take me but five minutes."

I waited two hours. During that time I imagined many things that they must have been discussing. Among other topics I was sure they were talking about me. I became very much upset. When my coworker did return she said, "Oh *Sensei*, I'm so sorry I kept you waiting all this time."

If only I had said, "Never mind, we'll go now," all would have gone smoothly. I could not say that because I was wrought up inside. I do not remember what I said, but I do know that it was something nasty.

God continued to deal with me about this failure. I saw that it was self-something I had not realized before. I saw that my commitment to God had not been complete. I found myself becoming impatient because there seemed to be so many difficulties to overcome.

A few days later I was reading Andrew Murray's book on humility. He wrote:

Humility is perfect quietness of heart. It is to have no trouble. It is never to be fretted, vexed, irritated, sore or disappointed. It is to expect nothing, to wonder at nothing that is done to me, to feel nothing done against me. It is to be at rest when nobody praises me, and when I am blamed and despised. It is to have a blessed home in the Lord where I can go in and shut the

door and kneel to my Father in secret.
I am at peace as in a deep sea of calm-
ness when all around is trouble.

Every word of this definition pierced my
heart. I had thought I was humble, but I
knew then that I did not know the first
thing about humility. I would get fretful,
vexed, sore and disappointed. I seemed to
be all undone.

Fight Against Impatience

Time and again I had to fight against this
great impatience of mine. Here is another
example. After I had moved to a large, ram-
bling house, I kept a box of pencils on a table in the entrance where I often stopped to
write down an address or some note that I
wanted to remember. One day I put another box there and said to the girls who
worked for me: "Now if you break the lead
of one of these pencils, please put it in this
second box." I explained that when I was in
a rush to write something it would enable
me to avoid picking up a pencil with no
lead. They said: "Oh, yes, we understand."

One morning not long after, a gentleman
came to the door. "I have only a minute,"

he said, "please take down this address." I rushed to the box of pencils. I picked up one pencil after another that had no lead. As I picked up the seventh pencil, the last one in the box, and saw the broken lead, I gave it an impatient toss. Then I found a pencil and wrote the address the man gave me; but immediately the Holy Spirit said, "I was grieved when you threw the pencil down in that manner."

After the man left, I called my helpers and said, "Girls, I want you to pray for me. I have grieved the Holy Spirit and it is no light thing." I told them what I had done; I wept and prayed. They wept and prayed. I did not say, "You put the pencils in the wrong box." That really had nothing to do with it. I had been impatient. I had acted in this way because of an impatient trait down inside that had to be dealt with.

I told the Lord about this, and I never have felt this impatient attitude from that day to this.

The Lord said, "When you see any working of this old self-nature, bring it to Me and I'll put it on the cross and it will be gone." It is very important when we are dealing with the traits of the *self-nature* that we do not make excuses for them or try to vindicate ourselves.

God Takes It to the Cross

No matter what comes up, God takes it to the cross when we let Him deal definitely with our old self-nature. God also said to me at that time, "I never let anything come into the life of My child unless I have a reason. I have undertaken to perfect you. I have undertaken to bring you into the place of complete deliverance. Everything I let come into your life is purposeful."

I learned not to ask why some things happened but, "What is God doing now? What is He trying to teach me through this particular situation?"

Another area in which God dealt with me was concerning selfishness and sensitivity. Some of us seem to have our nerves on the outside and we get hurt very easily. It is not the things that hurt; it is *you* that God wants to deal with! He wants to show you where self is residing. God let me go through more difficult experiences before I learned the spiritual lessons He wanted me to learn!

CHAPTER EIGHT

WHAT IF I HAVE A HYPERSENSITIVE, SUSPICIOUS NATURE?

*I will always be unhappy
until I yield it to God!*

I wonder if God ever had to deal with you because you were oversensitive in areas where you feel you were not properly "appreciated." This was one of my problem attitudes in Japan.

After my brother, Tom, came to Japan as a missionary, we decided that it was time to organize the Alliance church in Japan. We were happy to have a group of fine, educated men who seemed to be dedicated to the Lord. The church was organized and everything went smoothly and according to plan. But I began to feel very lonely and a little on the outside because I had less responsibility than before.

One Sunday morning when I went into the church, the pastor and one of the deacons who were engaged in conversation stopped talking as I entered. In my oversensitivity and desire to be noticed, I thought they did not want me to hear what they were saying; I felt very much left out.

So I asked the Lord: "What is the cause of this ugly feeling? Please show me!"

It was quite some days before the Lord revealed the reason. It came to me as I was reading Matthew 20:28: "Even as the Son of man came not to be ministered unto, but to minister, and to give his life a ransom for many." I had read that passage many times before. My reaction was: of course, I did not want to be served!

When people came to tie my shoes (we had to remove our shoes when we entered a house in Japan), I did not want them to do it. When people would give me a cushion, I knew they would sit on the bare floor. I did not need the cushion. I could sit on the bare floor too. I did not want to be served!

But the Holy Spirit showed me that although I did not expect people to wait on me physically, I did like them to minister to my old self-life. I liked them to say, "We are so glad you're here this morning; we wouldn't know what to do without you. We must have your opinion."

The Lord Jesus reminded me of His own ministry by saying, "I wasn't served, and after I had healed and blessed people, nobody said, 'Thank you.' Instead they gave Me a crown of thorns and a cross. They took My life. And I want you to follow in My footsteps. They are not going to thank you and you don't need thanks. Whenever there is something to do, do it gladly and then get out of the way."

Become Fertilizer

One day as I was praying, God showed me as in a vision a leaf fall to the ground and decay right before my eyes and become fertilizer for the tree. God said, "From now on I want you to become 'fertilizer' for this church." Now nobody goes around praising fertilizer. No one ever says, "What wonderful fertilizer!"

When I was in charge of the church, I did the things I wanted to do and gave the unwanted tasks to someone else. A leader can sometimes be very selfish. I was filled with deep conviction regarding my lack of the demonstration of the Holy Spirit. But then, when I cast myself upon God, glad hallelujahs filled my soul as He gave blessed release. "If the Son therefore shall make you free, ye shall be free indeed" (John 8:36).

From that time on it made no difference whether I performed the task or someone else did. I realized that it was God's work and that I really did not have anything to do with it except to obey Him.

God richly blessed the little church and caused it to grow.

CHAPTER NINE

WHAT ABOUT FALSE RUMORS AFFECTING MY REPUTATION?

"Not one word in defense"
and "Be ready to forgive!"

In many ways the Holy Spirit continued to probe deeper into my inner life.

Being a single lady and a missionary, I was very zealous to maintain a good reputation. One of the ladies in the mission wanted her husband to be president of the work. While my brother, who was president, was on furlough, she thought if she could get me off the field too, everything would be in her favor. In order to accomplish this she told a story that I was not living morally. She even wrote to the New York Board; they sent out a representative to check this report.

When I heard about this (someone is always kind enough to tell you when there is a rumor about you), the Lord instructed me: "You are not to say one word or try to vindicate yourself."

Oh, how I longed to say one word at least, but the Lord said, "Not one word! You are not even to let anyone know that you have heard the rumor. Your business in the midst of this is to die to self, even to your reputation."

I continually prayed, "Lord, give me grace." I was not very happy and neither was I rejoicing in the Lord. Matthew 5:11-12 says that when men speak evil against us, we should "rejoice, and be exceeding glad."

Although I went through this trial, I almost lost my health. I did not want to go out or to meet people because I wondered if they had heard the rumor.

"I Will; I Do"

I asked the Lord about this attitude and how I should react. His answer came to me one Sunday morning during a church service when a young man read Colossians 3:13: "Forbearing one another, and forgiving one another, if any man have a quarrel against any: even as Christ forgave you, so also do ye." The Japanese translation of the Scripture is very clear: "If any man have a cause to blame another, forgive him." As the Holy Spirit illumined the Word, I looked up to God and said, "Lord, I will, I do."

This experience not only upset me, but it brought to light envy, jealousy and suspicion that I didn't know were in my heart. Those traits were there—no question about that. Then the Lord Jesus said, "You didn't know but I knew, and I purposely brought this experience to you that you might see these traits."

I was deeply moved when I thought of the pains that God was taking to train and to teach me. I thanked Him for showing me this condition.

Self-Life Must Die

The Lord revealed to me that the Adamic nature—the self-life—must be met by death. I had thought that when I was cleansed by the blood of Jesus and filled with the Holy Spirit all the self-life was taken away. He showed me that His method of dealing with the self-life was not just cleansing; it was crucifixion.

Death of the old is necessary for new life and fruit. "Except a corn of wheat fall into the ground and die, it abideth alone: but if it die, it bringeth forth much fruit" (John 12:24). Oh, how these words pierced my soul! I said, "Lord Jesus, I don't know how to die." In desperation I cried, "Teach me to die!"

Again God spoke to me, this time through Matthew 16:24: "If any man will come after me [be my disciple], let him deny himself, and take up his cross, and follow me." I had never understood that passage. Many times I had asked what God meant by denying self. I knew He did not mean to deny my existence, for even if I said, "I am not here," I still was.

Now the meaning of this Scripture was clear to me: *self* should have no place whatever. Now I understood that *self* was to die. But I didn't know how to die! In my desperation I cried again, "Teach me to die!"

God's instructions were that every time there was an uprising of *self* I was to go to Him directly, immediately and without making any excuse whatever. I was to confess it to Him. I saw that I had been excusing myself for these traits and actions.

Sometimes when you get angry with someone, you say, "I know I shouldn't have, but they shouldn't have done what they did either!" You don't get anywhere that way. But if you take the matter to the Lord, He will take it away. When someone hurts you, bring it immediately to God. Do not take time to tell your best friend before bringing it to the Lord.

God said, "I'll bring experiences into your life that are necessary for you to see where *self* is hiding. You are unable to see *self* but I will show you."

God knows every place where *self* works in our lives. It seemed to me at this time that every part of my being was stained with this old self. God exposed one trait after another, showed it to me and brought it to the cross.

When you really forgive a wrong, it is gone. True forgiveness does not put it away on the shelf to bring out at some other time. When I said, "I do forgive," I was liberated. Gone was the feeling of sensitivity about meeting people. Gone was the resentment toward those who had hurt me.

Unutterable joy filled my soul with this blessed release! It is wonderful to be forgiven, but it is more wonderful to forgive.

Still, though this was a blessed victory, it was not the end. But knowing that I was in the will of God made me very happy.

CHAPTER TEN

HOW CAN I KNOW
THAT SELF HAS
GONE TO THE CROSS?

*Ask God in humility for His
revelation of resurrection life.*

Shortly after this experience, feeling the need to be alone and rest, I went up to Karuizawa, a place in the mountains where many people went to escape the heat of the lowlands. It was October and the summer people had gone. I seemed to have the whole mountain to myself. God came to me so wonderfully with the promise in Zephaniah 3:17: "The LORD thy God in the midst of thee is mighty; he will save."

I had previously thought this verse meant that He was in the midst of the church. But He said, "No, I'm in the midst of *you*; I have come as your indwelling God, and My resurrection life is flowing through every nerve of your body, every organ. Just trust Me." I kept repeating His promise over and over—and believing it. He so perfectly healed me that I scarcely realized I had a nerve in my body!

I waited much on the Lord, but still the self-life bothered me.

Satan tormented me greatly in those days, saying, "Yes, you thought that if you stayed in Japan after the Board withdrew its support and trusted God and were a glory to Him, everything would be all right. You will go home a nervous wreck and it will be the end of you."

His satanic screams were so loud that I would leave the house and walk up the mountain. From the top of the mountain I would cry out to the limit of my voice, "I will not doubt. All you devils in hell, listen! I will not *doubt*! My God will make Himself known to the Japanese people through me!"

One morning when I was walking on the mountain, God spoke to me with such clarity that even now it seems I can see the spot where I was when He said, *I will dwell in you and walk in you.* "I—the living God—I will live with you and walk with you. It is not going to be you anymore; it will be I" (2 Corinthians 6:16, paraphrased). How my heart rejoiced at these precious words!

When I arose the next morning, I decided to fast and pray. During this time of waiting on the Lord, He gave me these wonderful words: "For if we have been planted together in the likeness of his death, we shall be also in the likeness of his resurrection" (Romans 6:5).

Self Had Gone to the Cross

In the depths of my soul I knew that *self* had gone to the cross. I had been planted in the likeness of His death and was living in His resurrection power. Jesus Himself in His resurrection glory stepped with new fullness into the throne of my heart. How I rejoiced over this victory in Christ! I had the assurance of these words: "I in them, and thou in me, that they may be made perfect in one" (John 17:23).

After this experience I returned to my work. Everything was different! Indeed, everything has been different ever since. Galatians 2:20 became reality. "I am crucified with Christ: nevertheless I live; yet not I, but *Christ liveth in me"* (emphasis added).

It was a new revelation to me that as I actually entered into Christ's death, I also entered into His resurrection. Dr. A.B. Simpson wrote a hymn that we often sing:

Yes, I'm living in the glory
    As He promised in His Word;
I am dwelling in the heavenlies,
    Living in the glory of the Lord.

One Sunday morning as I stepped into the church, God gave me another illuminating revelation, this time from Romans 7:4: "Wherefore, my brethren, ye also are become dead to the law by the body of Christ; that ye should be married to another, even to him who is raised from the dead, that we should bring forth fruit unto God."

All through the service God was saying: "Through the offering of My body you are made dead to the *old self* that you might be joined to another." I saw that through this new relationship, I had come to inherit all. His death was mine; His burial was mine; his resurrection was mine; his ascension was mine. He transferred all of this to me. I was to live in heavenly places in Christ.

I had always thought that when I died or when Jesus returns I (as a part of His Church) would become His bride. He revealed to me that I am now His bride. I am already joined to Him. "I am the vine," said Jesus, "ye are the branches" (John 15:5). Nothing or no one can separate me from this precious union.

This is how an old hymn expresses it:

His forever, only His;
   Who the Lord and me shall part?
Ah, with what a rest of bliss,
   Christ can fill the trusting heart!
Heaven and earth may fade and flee,
   Firstborn light in gloom decline;
But while God and I shall be,
   I am His, and He is mine!

See God's Glory Only

As God continued to teach me, He made very real Matthew 6:22: "The light of the body is the eye: if therefore thine eye be single, thy whole body shall be full of light." I was very conscious that I did not have a single eye, an eye to see God's glory only. I wanted a little glory myself. The cry of my heart was that of Gerhard Tersteegen when he wrote:

Jesus, Thy boundless love to me
  No thought can reach, no tongue
    declare;
Oh, knit my thankful heart to Thee.
  And reign without a rival there!

At the same time I was conscious that there was a rival, much as I hated it—even self.

God teaches us in Luke 11:36: "If thy whole body therefore be full of light, having no part dark, the whole shall be full of light, as when the bright shining of a candle doth give thee light." When self went to the cross I knew that no part was left dark. It seemed as if a glorious light had been turned on in my inner soul!

CHAPTER ELEVEN

WHAT MAY BE THE MOST DIFFICULT LESSON EN ROUTE TO VICTORY?

*To face the fact that even my
good traits must go to the cross!*

Beloved, here is something that is very hard for us to see on our path to spiritual victory:

Even our seeming good traits must go to the cross!

Many people thought they were being kind when they would say, "Miss Francis is such a loving person"—and I believed it, too!

It is true that I did many pleasant things. But God said, "Yes, you are very loving, but the trouble is you love yourself."

I was astonished. What did He mean?

117

At that time three girls lived with me. They should have been strong Christians, but they were spoiled. The Lord said to me: "You are like a mother who is spoiling her child. She thinks she loves the child if she gives her everything she wants. It is not that she loves the child but that it pleases her to do this." This vivid portrayal pierced my inner being like an arrow. I pleaded earnestly, "Lord, what can I do?"

He said, "Consign it to the cross."

From that moment on there was a tremendous difference in my life. This trait seemed to be the center of my self-life. So I learned that my self-life was not always some ugly thing, some mean thing. With true insight into my human spirit, God knew that I had been brought up in a loving home and that it pleased me to do nice things. He had put His finger on the root of my weakness—myself!

Self Has to Be Denied

So self, whether good or bad, had to be denied. I cast myself on the Lord, filled with deep conviction of my lack of oneness with Him. Again He proved Himself my strong Deliverer. Since that day that attitude in my heart has been different toward everyone. I recognized immediately when dealing with people that this trait of pleasing self was gone. In times just when I had been talking to someone I liked and someone interrupted us, I had an inner uprising within me. Complete deliverance was now mine; interruptions were accepted as from the Lord.

As I entered into Christ's death, it was as the Apostle Paul wrote: "I am crucified with Christ: nevertheless I live; yet not I, but Christ liveth in me: and the life which I now live in the flesh I live by the faith of the Son of God, who loved me, and gave himself for me" (Galatians 2:20). He lives within. Oh, the blessedness of this relationship with the risen Christ in all His fullness!

His death had become my death; His burial had become mine; His resurrection had become mine; His ascension had become mine. I now live in heavenly places in Christ—the result of inwardly surrendering everything to Jesus.

Another experience that God used in leading me into this blessed mystery of the indwelling Christ came one day when a group of Japanese young people and I were singing that wonderful hymn by George Matheson:

> Make me a captive, Lord,
>   And then I shall be free;
> Force me to render up my sword,
>   And I shall conqueror be.

All at once God revealed to me that when anything struck against me I would immediately take a vindictive stand.

The words of the hymn so overwhelmed me that I had to go into another room and kneel before the Lord. I cried out to Him: "I have sung this song so many times before, but I never realized I had a sword. Lord, I surrender it to Thee." Gently He took it. Later, I realized I had no sword from that time onward.

CHAPTER TWELVE

WHEN CAN I EXPECT FULL VICTORY OVER SELF?

*When the resurrected Christ
has taken over without a rival!*

Many people who come forward in our services indicate that they are troubled by some outcropping of the old life of self.

I have sometimes asked them, "What do you do when these uprisings of self come?" Invariably their answer has been that they felt they had failed God. They had felt downcast and had wept and repented until peace came. I knew about this so well from my own experiences. But this is God showing us "self" for a purpose. This is cause for thankfulness. Self is not sin and will continue with us. We were born with this nature and we are not responsible for its failures. However, we are responsible if we let self, rather than the blessed Holy Spirit, take over and control us.

It seems natural to expect a wonderful, miraculous and instantaneous deliverance. "Step by step you will be delivered," were God's words to me. Isaiah 1:25 became very real: "And I will turn my hand upon thee, and purely purge away thy dross, and take away all thy tin." In the final analysis, deliverance was instantaneously effective when He entered all the doors I opened to Him to take over my entire life!

For so long I did not know that the life of victory I now live was possible. In fact, had someone told me, I could not have understood the blessed reality of "forever one with Him." I believe the greatest day of my life, except for salvation, was when I knew that the resurrected Christ had really taken over without a rival—that He was Lord of all in my whole being.

Oh, the rest of soul! All is His and He is mine forever and forever. No words can express the joy and peace of the heart in which Christ dwells as Lord.

John 15 teaches about the abiding life. As the branch we draw sustenance and strength from the vine—the Lord Jesus.

Fruitfulness arises spontaneously from this abiding in the vine.

Have you experienced this reality? God will satisfy every desire that He puts in your heart. Your longings for Him will be fully satisfied. The words of Tersteegen's hymn offers praise to Him who is worthy:

> But I tell you I have seen Him,
>   God's beloved Son,
> From His lips have learned the
>   mystery
>   He and His are one.
> There, as knit into the body
>   Every joint and limb,
> We, His ransomed, His beloved,
>   We are one with Him.

Hebrews 4:9-10 is a meaningful passage: "There remaineth therefore a rest to the people of God. For he that is entered into his rest, he also hath *ceased from his own works*, as God did from his" (emphasis added). We can never enter into this marvelous rest as long as self has any place in our hearts. *Self* is an enemy within the camp. But oh, the joy when we can say from the heart:

Day by day His tender mercy
   Healing, helping, full and free,
Sweet and strong, and oh, so patient,
Brought me lower while I whispered,
   "Less of self and more of Thee."

Higher than the highest heavens,
   Deeper than the deepest sea,
Lord, Thy love at last hath conquered:
Grant me now my spirit's longing,
   None of self and all of Thee.

Books by A.W. Tozer:

The Attributes of God
The Attributes of God Journal
The Best of A.W. Tozer Vol. 1
The Best of A.W. Tozer Vol. 2
Born after Midnight
The Christian Book of Mystical Verse
Christ the Eternal Son
The Counselor
The Early Tozer: A Word in Season
Echoes from Eden
Faith Beyond Reason
Gems from Tozer
God Tells the Man Who Cares
How to Be Filled with the Holy Spirit
I Call It Heresy!
I Talk Back to the Devil
Jesus, Author of Our Faith
Jesus Is Victor
Jesus, Our Man in Glory
Let My People Go, A biography of Robert A. Jaffray
Man: The Dwelling Place of God
Men Who Met God
The Next Chapter after the Last
Of God and Men
Paths to Power
The Price of Neglect
The Pursuit of God
The Pursuit of God: A 31-Day Experience
The Pursuit of Man (formerly *The Divine Conquest*)
The Quotable Tozer
The Quotable Tozer II

Renewed Day by Day, Vol. 1
Renewed Day by Day, Vol. 2
The Root of the Righteous
Rut, Rot or Revival
The Set of the Sail
The Size of the Soul
Success and the Christian
That Incredible Christian
This World: Playground or Battleground?
The Tozer CD-Rom Library
Tozer on the Holy Spirit
Tozer on Worship and Entertainment
The Tozer Pulpit (in two volumes)
Tozer Speaks to Students
Tozer Topical Reader
Tragedy in the Church: The Missing Gifts
The Warfare of the Spirit
We Travel an Appointed Way
Whatever Happened to Worship?
Who Put Jesus on the Cross?
Wingspread, A biography of A.B. Simpson

Books by R. Mabel Francis:

One Shall Chase a Thousand
Filled with the Spirit . . . Then What?